P9-AQK-830

Americans from the Caribbean and Central America

by Jayne Keedle

Series Consultant: Judith A. Warner, Ph.D.,
Professor of Sociology and Criminal Justice,
Texas A&M International University

Marshall Cavendish
Benchmark
New York

Marshall Cavendish Benchmark
99 White Plains Road
Tarrytown, NY 10591
www.marshallcavendish.us

Library of Congress Cataloging-in-Publication Data

Keedle, Jayne.
    Americans from the Caribbean and Central America / by Jayne Keedle.
       p. cm. — (New Americans)
    Includes bibliographical references and index.
    ISBN 978-0-7614-4302-5
  1. Caribbean Americans—Juvenile literature. 2. Central American
Americans—Juvenile literature. I. Title.
    E184.C27K44 2010
    305.868'728—dc22   2009003171

Developed for Marshall Cavendish Benchmark by RJF Publishing LLC
Robert Famighetti, President
www.RJFpublishing.com
Design: Westgraphix LLC/Tammy West
Photo Research: Edward A. Thomas
Map Illustrator: Stefan Chabluk
Index: Nila Glikin

Photo credits: Cover, 1, 63, 67: Getty Images; 5, 12, 13, 22, 25, 26, 32, 35, 39, 43, 50, 54,
57, 60, 62, 68: AP/Wide World Photos; 6, 64: © Jeff Greenberg/Alamy; 10, 52: © Richard
Levine/Alamy; 18: © Bettmann/CORBIS; 20: The Granger Collection, New York; 28: National
Geographic/Getty Images; 44: AFP/Getty Images; 58: CBS/Photofest; 66: © CLAUDIA DAUT/
Reuters/Corbis.

Cover: People enjoy the annual Calle Ocho celebration in the Little Havana
neighborhood of Miami, Florida.

Printed in Malaysia.

135642

CONTENTS

Words defined in the glossary are in **bold** type
the first time they appear in the text.

INTRODUCTION

The United States has embraced immigration for most of its history—and has been a destination of choice for people seeking a better life. Today hundreds of thousands of immigrants arrive each year to live and work and make their way in a new country. These "New Americans" come for many reasons, and they come from places all over the world. They bring with them new customs, languages, and traditions—and face many challenges in their adopted country. Over time, they and their children are changed by and become part of the American mainstream culture. At the same time, the mainstream is itself changed as it absorbs many elements of the immigrants' cultures, from ethnic foods to ideas from non-Western belief systems. An understanding of the New Americans, and how they will form part of the American future, is essential for everyone.

This series focuses on recent immigrants from eight major countries and regions: the Caribbean and Central America, China, India and other South Asian countries, Korea, Mexico, Russia and Eastern Europe, Southeast Asia, and West Africa.

Each of these geographic areas is a major source of the millions of immigrants who have come to the United States in the last decades of the twentieth century and the beginning of the twenty-first. For many of these people, the opportunity to move to the United States was opened up by the major

New Americans being sworn in as U.S. citizens.

changes in U.S. immigration law that occurred in the 1960s. For others, the opportunity or imperative to immigrate was triggered by events in their own countries, such as the collapse of Communism in Eastern Europe or civil wars in Central America.

Some of the New Americans found sizable communities of Americans from the same ethnic background and had the benefit of "ethnic neighborhoods" to move into where they could feel welcome and get help adjusting to American life. Many of these communities originated in a previous major wave of immigration, from the 1880s to 1920. Some of the New Americans found very few predecessors to ease the transition as they faced the challenges of adjustment.

These volumes tell the stories of the New Americans, including the personal accounts of a number of immigrants and their children who agreed to be interviewed by some of the authors. As you read, you will learn about the countries of origin and the cultures of these newcomers to American society. You will learn, as well, about how the New Americans are enriching, as they adapt to, American life.

Judith A. Warner, Ph.D.
Professor of Sociology and Criminal Justice
Texas A&M International University

A group of men enjoy a game of dominoes in Maximo Gomez Park in Miami's Cuban-American Little Havana neighborhood. A mural of leaders who attended a Summit of the Americas meeting is in the background.

CHAPTER ONE

THE CARIBBEAN AND CENTRAL AMERICAN COMMUNITY TODAY

Miami's Little Havana neighborhood is as close to Cuba as most Americans will ever be. Florida's best-known Cuban-American district stretches for fifteen blocks along Calle Ocho (Eighth Street). Restaurants serve Cuban favorites—shredded beef, plantains, and black beans and rice. In storefront factories, skilled workers roll cigars by hand. At sidewalk stalls, passersby stop for cups of strong Cuban coffee.

Cuban heroes are honored with statues at a memorial park just off Calle Ocho. They are well-remembered by locals, some of whom leave offerings for them at the foot of a tree. In Maximo Gomez Park, a large mural of the 1994 **Summit of the Americas** (held in Miami) adds a splash of color. Locals call this Domino Park. It's where some Cuban Americans meet for serious games of dominoes. Spanish (the language of Cuba) is the language spoken here. Music is part of life on Calle Ocho. The sound of Cuban salsa, mambo, and hip-hop-influenced timba music throbs from open doors and passing cars. Drums thump like the heartbeat of the district. If home is where the heart is, then many Cuban Americans are home here.

Caribbean Immigrants

Cuban Americans make up a large and well-established **nationality group** in the United States. The U.S. Census Bureau estimated that in 2006 there were more than 1.5 million Cuban Americans (people born in Cuba or whose parents, grandparents, or other ancestors were born in Cuba), more than from any other Caribbean country. Two-thirds of all Cuban Americans were living in Florida. Particularly in the southern part of the state, many communities besides Little Havana (which is named for Havana, the capital of Cuba) have a Cuban flavor.

The second-largest Caribbean nationality group is made up of people who immigrated from or trace their ancestry to the Dominican Republic. In 2006, there were about 1.2 million Dominican Americans in the United States. More than half of them were living in New York, and many others lived in New Jersey or Florida. In Dominican neighborhoods in New York City, restaurants and shops feature Dominican foods, and Spanish (the language of the Dominican Republic) is spoken in many stores and businesses. Such neighborhoods can be comfortable communities for many new immigrants from the Dominican Republic.

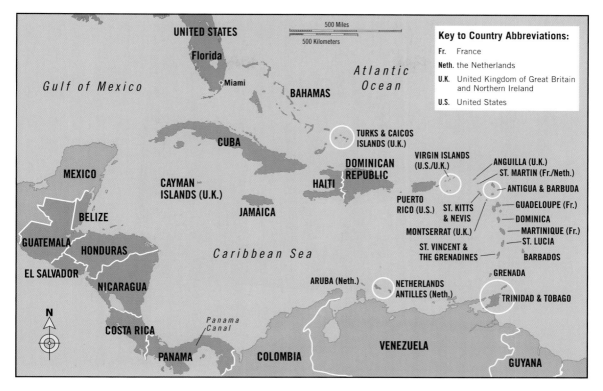

Many people have come to the United States from the nearby islands of the Caribbean and countries of Central America.

Cubans and Dominicans aren't the only people who have come to the United States from the Caribbean. In fact, the closeness of the United States has attracted people from islands throughout the region. Many of the Caribbean islands are known collectively as the West Indies. The West Indies essentially form an arc, moving south from Florida to South America, which separates the Caribbean Sea to the west from the Atlantic Ocean to the east. The northern-most islands of the West Indies are the Bahamas. South of the Bahamas are the Greater Antilles, including the islands of Cuba, Jamaica, Hispaniola (which contains the countries

Washington Heights is one of several
neighborhoods in New York City with a
large Dominican-American population.

of Haiti and the Dominican Republic), and Puerto Rico. Farther south are the Lesser Antilles, a large number of smaller islands, including the Virgin Islands (very near Puerto Rico) and, close to South America, Trinidad and Tobago. The name West Indies was given because Christopher Columbus, the first European to see the islands, was trying to find India when he first saw them.

Although the islands of the Caribbean are grouped together geographically, their cultures can be quite different from one another. Because the islands were colonized by various European countries, the languages spoken on different islands include Dutch, French (including in Haiti), and English (including in Jamaica), as well as Spanish. On many

Hispaniola: One Island, Two Stories

Hispaniola is one island divided into two countries. The western side of the island is Haiti. The eastern side is the Dominican Republic. The two countries share ancient history. The island was home to the Arawak people for thousands of years before Christopher Columbus arrived in 1492. Columbus, who sailed for the king and queen of Spain, named the island Hispaniola and founded the first Spanish settlements there. Eventually, most Spanish settlers were concentrated on the eastern part of the island.

In the 1600s, French and other European settlers arrived in western Hispaniola. Wars in Europe resulted in Spain signing over this western part to France in 1697. That split the island into two parts. The French part was populated mostly by African slaves. The Spanish part was populated mostly by people of mixed Indian, Spanish, and African ancestry.

A century later, a former slave named Toussaint Louverture led a successful rebellion and assumed control of Haiti. He freed all the slaves and proclaimed himself governor. Although he failed to hold onto control for long, the rebellion did lead to independence from France in 1804.

Haiti was the first country to be founded by former slaves. General Jean-Jacques Dessalines, a Haitian who led the rebels against a French army, became its first president.

Haitians briefly gained control of the entire island in the 1820s, but the Spanish-speaking Dominicans in eastern Hispaniola successfully rebelled in 1844. Since that time, except for a brief period of Spanish rule in the 1860s, the Dominican Republic has been an independent country.

The differences in language and ancestry between the two parts of Hispaniola continued to be a source of friction after Dominican independence. Haiti and the Dominican Republic may be geographically close, but they view themselves as being quite different.

islands, these European languages have blended with West African languages originally spoken by slaves brought to the Caribbean by the European colonizers. The combination languages, sometimes called Creoles, can be difficult for anyone but island locals to understand. Some Caribbean islands are still territories of European countries, and Puerto Rico is part of the United States. But the Caribbean today has many independent countries. Many people in the Caribbean have mixed ancestry—that is, their ancestors may include Europeans, Africans, and the original inhabitants of the region (the Arawak Indians, also called Taino, and the Carib Indians, for whom the region is named).

Puerto Rico, "La Isla Bonita"

Although Puerto Rico is a Caribbean island, people who move from Puerto Rico to the U.S. mainland are not immigrants. That is because Puerto Rico is part of the United States and Puerto Ricans are U.S. citizens. Someone who moves from Puerto Rico to, say, New York is no more an immigrant than someone who moves from New Jersey to New York.

The first European settlement on Puerto Rico was started by Christopher Columbus, who claimed the island for Spain in 1493. It remained a Spanish possession until the United States defeated Spain in the Spanish-American War in 1898. In the treaty ending that war, Spain granted Puerto Rico to the United States.

Culturally, Puerto Rico continues to have much in common with other former Spanish colonies in the Caribbean, and Spanish is the first language of most people on the island. The island's nickname is "La Isla Bonita," Spanish for "beautiful island."

In 2006, according to the Census Bureau, about 3.7 million people lived in Puerto Rico, and about an equal number of Puerto Ricans lived elsewhere in the United States, including more than one million in New York and almost 700,000 in Florida.

Spectators enjoy the annual Puerto Rican Day parade in New York City.

Destruction from power-
ful hurricanes adds to Haiti's economic
woes. Three storms in three weeks hit Haiti in 2008,
causing widespread flooding and more than a hundred deaths.

After Cubans and Dominicans, the largest Caribbean-American communities are Jamaican Americans (more than 900,000 people) and Haitian Americans (more than 750,000). More Jamaican Americans live in New York—over 300,000—than in any other state, closely followed by Florida, home to more than 250,000 Jamaican Americans. Almost half of all Haitian Americans (more than 366,000 people) live in Florida.

Because Florida is so close to the Caribbean, it is not surprising that many **immigrants** from that region enter the United States in Florida. Many of them choose to stay there.

Some may join relatives or friends. Others simply find it helpful to join existing communities of people from their native country—where language, food, and customs are familiar and where people and organizations may assist newcomers in adjusting to life in a new country.

People from the Caribbean come to the United States for a variety of reasons. Many are simply seeking more economic opportunity and a chance for a more comfortable life, since the economies of many Caribbean countries are not strong. Haiti, for example, is one of the poorest countries in the world. Most Caribbean countries, even if better off than Haiti, are not as **affluent** as the United States. Economic problems can be aggravated by the powerful and destructive hurricanes that hit the Caribbean. Some countries in the region have a history of—or at least recent periods of—rule by **dictators** or political violence. So some immigrants have come to the United States for greater freedom or for safety from political enemies or political chaos. Most Cuban immigrants have come to the United States since Fidel Castro established a **Communist** government in Cuba in 1959, in many cases for a combination of political and economic reasons.

Immigrants from Central America

In 2006, according to the Census Bureau, almost 3.4 million people in the United States were of Central American heritage—about two-thirds of them were born in Central America, and about one-third had parents, grandparents, or other ancestors who were born there. Most immigrants

States with the Most Americans from Central America

California	1,058,151
Florida	399,411
Texas	371,497
New York	294,922
Virginia	147,775
New Jersey	146,191
Maryland	130,760
Georgia	87,516
North Carolina	78,833
Massachussetts	76,309

Source: U.S. Bureau of the Census, 2006 estimates

15

from Central America settle in California, Texas, Florida, or New York. As many as 560,000 Central Americans live in the Los Angeles area. Central Americans also make up about 10 percent of the foreign-born population living in Washington, D.C., Maryland, and Virginia.

Most Central American immigrants are recent arrivals. Almost 30 percent of immigrants from Central America have come to the United States since the year 2000. A slightly larger number arrived in the 1990s.

People from El Salvador represent the largest group in the Central American community. The Census Bureau estimated that there were almost 1.4 million Salvadoran Americans in 2006. In that year there were also almost 875,000 Guatemalan Americans and almost half a million Honduran Americans.

Actual figures may be higher than Census Bureau estimates. As many as half of all foreign-born Central Americans in the United States may be **undocumented immigrants**. That means they do not have **visas**—the official U.S. government documents that allow immigrants to live and work in the United States—and entered the country without official authorization. Concerned about being forcibly returned to their native countries, undocumented immigrants are very often reluctant to give information to census takers.

Like people from the Caribbean, Central Americans have come to the United States for a combination of political and economic reasons. In the second half of the twentieth century, most good agricultural land was owned by a small number of foreign companies and other wealthy landowners. On large plantations, they grew such crops as bananas, coffee, and sugar for export, while the people who worked the land received low wages and lived in poverty. At the same time, military dictators controlled most Central American governments. They often brutally put down groups that opposed the government and stopped workers' efforts to organize unions to improve their wages and working conditions. The result was bloody civil wars in several Central American countries. By the early twenty-first century, economies had improved somewhat, and Central American countries had democratic governments. Still, most countries remained poor, and many people saw immigration as the only hope for a better life.

Central America: An Overview

Central America, the narrow strip of land connecting Mexico and South America, has seven countries today. They are Belize, Guatemala, Honduras, El Salvador, Nicaragua, Costa Rica, and Panama. The region was once the heart of the Mayan empire. This ancient Indian civilization—known for its magnificent palaces and pyramids and for its achievements in astronomy and engineering—reached the height of its power between C.E. 250 and 900. Spectacular Mayan ruins have been discovered in many parts of Central America, particularly in Belize and Guatemala. The Maya still live in the region to this day.

Except for what is now Belize, Central America was colonized by Spain in the sixteenth century. That gives most of the region a common culture and language—Spanish. Costa Rica, El Salvador, Honduras, Guatemala, Nicaragua, and Panama all gained independence from Spain in 1821. Panama became part of the neighboring South American country of Colombia until the beginning of the twentieth century. In 1903, the United States helped Panama gain its independence from Colombia, and in return the new government allowed the United States to build the Panama Canal across the country, connecting the Atlantic and Pacific oceans. The United States controlled the canal and the land immediately around it (the Panama Canal Zone) until returning them to Panama in the 1990s.

A former British colony (then called British Honduras), Belize became independent in 1981. English is the official language, but many people in Belize also speak Spanish, Mayan, and Creole.

U.S. Marines on patrol in Nicaragua in 1931. For most of the twentieth century, the United States was heavily involved in Central American affairs, and at times, this involvement had a major impact on immigration.

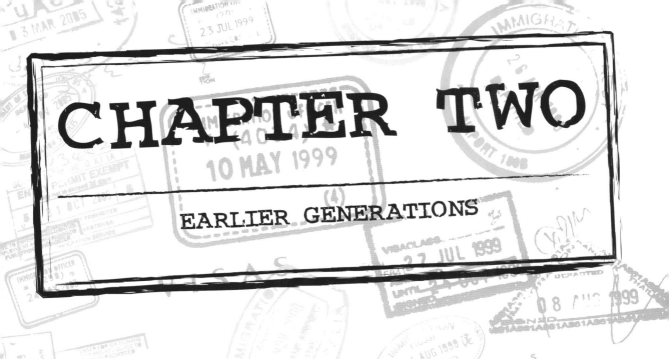

CHAPTER TWO

EARLIER GENERATIONS

There is a long history of people coming from the Caribbean to what is now the United States. But for centuries, most of these people did not come willingly—they were slaves. From the 1500s to the early 1800s, European and other slave traders brought millions of African slaves to the Caribbean. Most of them were forced to work on Caribbean plantations and in Caribbean mines under terrible conditions.

Many slaves, however, were sold to white Americans, mostly plantation owners in the South. In 1808, U.S. law made it illegal to import slaves into the United States, but some smuggling of slaves continued after that, until slavery itself became illegal throughout the United States at the end of the Civil War. The Thirteenth Amendment to the U.S. Constitution officially abolished slavery in December 1865.

Olaudah Equiano (c. 1745–1797)

Olaudah Equiano was the son of a Nigerian tribal leader. When he was about ten years old, Equiano was kidnapped from his African home in 1755. First, he was taken to the Caribbean island of Barbados. From there, he was shipped to Virginia, where he became the slave of an officer in the British Navy. In 1766, he bought his freedom. He moved to London and became an active **abolitionist**, working to end the slave trade. In 1789, he published his life story in the book *The Interesting Narrative of the Life of Olaudah Equiano, or Gustavus Vassa the African*. The book became a best-seller in England.

An illustration of Olaudah Equiano after he moved to London.

The Monroe Doctrine

Since the early 1800s, the United States has claimed a special interest in events in the countries of the Western Hemisphere, including the Caribbean and Central America, and asserted a right to prevent European or other foreign interference in those countries. This policy, known as the Monroe Doctrine, was expressed by U.S. President James Monroe in a message to Congress on December 2, 1823. In it, he warned European powers not to meddle in the political affairs of countries in the Western Hemisphere. Anything that happened in, for example, neighboring Central America or the Caribbean was a U.S. concern, and the United

States would take action if its interests or security were threatened.

For most of the nineteenth century, the United States was not really a powerful enough country to enforce the Monroe Doctrine. But by the early twentieth century, the United States had become a world power. The Monroe Doctrine then became a justification for the United States to become heavily involved in the politics of Central America and the Caribbean. The U.S. government supported leaders who cooperated with U.S. security, political, and business needs. Some of those leaders, however, did little to benefit their own people. Leaders who were seen as a threat to U.S. interests were often removed, by force if necessary. Sometimes, the U.S. military became directly involved. For example, U.S. Marines were stationed in Nicaragua almost continuously from 1912 to 1933 to help ensure that governments friendly to the United States would be in power. In the later decades of the twentieth century, active U.S. involvement in the politics of Central America and the Caribbean would at times have a major impact on immigration.

Earlier, in the 1940s, World War II had an impact on immigration. After the United States entered the war in 1941,

President James Monroe's Statement

In his message to Congress on December 2, 1823, President James Monroe said the following:

"It is only when our rights are invaded, or seriously [threatened], that we resent injuries, or make preparation for our defense. With the movements in this hemisphere, we are . . . more immediately connected. The political system of the [European] powers is essentially different . . . from that of America. . . . We should consider any attempt on their part to extend their system [of government] to any portion of this hemisphere, as dangerous to our peace and safety."

Fidel Castro at a rally in Havana in March 1959, shortly after he came to power.

millions of men joined the armed forces, and there was a shortage of workers for American factories and other businesses. Legislation passed by Congress allowed people from Jamaica, other islands in the West Indies, and British Honduras to enter the United States as temporary workers. By the end of the war in 1945, Caribbean workers were employed in more than thirty states. Although they were intended to be temporary workers, many simply stayed on in the United States.

Communism Comes to Cuba

Cuba was once a popular destination for American tourists. Many U.S. companies owned and operated businesses in Cuba. The Cuban Revolution changed all that. In 1959, Cuban dictator Fulgencio Batista was overthrown. The revolution was led by Fidel Castro and supported by many Cubans. Under Batista, most of the nation's wealth was in the hands of only a few powerful people. The majority of Cubans were extremely poor. The revolution aimed to change that. Castro believed that creating a Communist government was the best way to improve people's lives.

In 1959, there were about 124,000 Cuban Americans living in the United States. In the years immediately following the Cuban Revolution, that number almost doubled. Most of the new Cuban immigrants had been well off economically. They were professionals and businesspeople who did not want to live under a Communist government. Allowed to enter the United States as **refugees**, they headed for Florida in most cases, and they found a warm welcome in Miami. This wave of Cuban immigrants of the early 1960s is sometimes referred to as the "golden exiles." They were given assistance with resettling in the United States. In many cases, they had professional skills or experience in business. Many of them became economically successful in their new country and helped establish thriving Cuban-American communities, especially in Miami and elsewhere in South Florida.

Events in Cuba became tied up with the cold war, which began in 1945 and lasted for some forty-five years, between the United States and the Union of Soviet Socialist Republics, or Soviet Union—the world's two most powerful countries at that time. In the cold war, the United States and Soviet Union did not actually fight each other. Instead, the cold war was a struggle for influence in and control over countries in all parts of the world. The Soviet Union had a Communist government and tried to expand Communism to other countries. The United States was determined to stop the spread of Communism. Because of how close the Caribbean and Central America are to the United States, the U.S. government considered any Communist government in that region of the world to be a particular threat to U.S. national security.

Relations between the United States and Castro quickly became strained. The Cuban government took over American-owned businesses in Cuba. The United States stopped buying sugar from Cuba (sugar was the country's major crop and major export) and soon stopped almost all trade with Cuba. Cuba began receiving economic aid and then military aid from the Soviet Union. In the early 1960s, the U.S. Central Intelligence Agency (CIA) apparently attempted to have Castro assassinated. In 1961, the CIA supported the Bay of Pigs invasion. This was an invasion of Cuba in an attempt to overthrow Castro by a group of Cuban exiles (Cubans who had left the country after the revolution). The exiles, who landed at a spot known as the Bay of Pigs, were quickly defeated by Cuban forces.

In 1962, Castro agreed to let the Soviet Union build a base in Cuba for missiles armed with nuclear weapons. The missiles would be located just 90 miles (145 kilometers) from the coast of Florida and, if fired, could easily hit targets in the United States. When the United States found out about the missiles, it demanded that they be removed and the base destroyed, and U.S. Navy ships set up a blockade around Cuba to prevent Soviet missiles from being delivered. For several days during what became known as the Cuban missile crisis, the United States and the Soviet Union

At a United Nations meeting during the 1962
Cuban missile crisis, the United States showed
photographs taken from a spy plane of
the Soviet missile base in Cuba.

were on the brink of nuclear war. Ultimately, the Soviet Union did agree to remove all missiles, after the United States secretly agreed not to invade Cuba.

After the Cuban missile crisis, relations between the United States and Cuba continued to be strained. In subsequent decades, U.S.-Cuba tensions would continue to bring many Cubans to the United States.

Cubans trying to get to the United States arrive
safely in Key West, Florida, in 1980. They were
among the 125,000 people who left Cuba that year
in what became known as the Mariel boatlift.

CHAPTER THREE

THE NEW IMMIGRANTS

I n the mid–1960s the United States made major changes in its immigration laws. Previous law had set **quotas** on the number of immigrants who could enter the United States each year based on a person's country of origin. These quotas greatly favored immigrants from certain countries in Europe. The Immigration and Nationality Act of 1965 dramatically changed the rules. Although it set overall ceilings on the number of immigrants from the Eastern Hemisphere and the Western Hemisphere, it now gave priority to immigrants, not on their country of origin, but based in large part on whether they had needed occupational skills or whether they were joining family members in the United States. This new law paved the way for increased immigration from many countries outside of Europe.

Besides people receiving immigrant visas, many others entered the United States as refugees in the late twentieth century. And large numbers of undocumented immigrants entered the country as well.

Jamaican "Brain Drain"

In the 1970s and 1980s, Jamaica's economy had very serious problems. The 1970s was also a time of political unrest and rising crime rates in Jamaica. Since the United States had made immigration easier

Severe poverty has been one reason for Jamaican immigration to the United States. This street is in Jamaica's capital city, Kingston.

and Great Britain (the former colonial ruler of Jamaica) had made immigration for people from the West Indies more difficult, hundreds of thousands of Jamaicans decided to immigrate to the United States.

The new immigrants included many well-educated professionals, including doctors, lawyers, and people with scientific, technical, and business management skills. Their occupational skills were needed in the United States, and they saw much more opportunity for themselves, and a safer environment, in the United States than in their native country. Jamaica suffered from serious shortages of doctors, business managers, and other types of professionals because so many people had left. This kind of large-scale movement of skilled professionals out of a country is sometimes referred to as a "brain drain."

Immigrants from Jamaica also included many people who were not highly educated professionals but still saw more opportunity for themselves in the United States. And it included undocumented immigrants as well as those with immigrant visas. Immigration from Jamaica has continued in more recent decades but at somewhat lower levels.

The Mariel Boatlift

Most of the first Cuban immigrants of the early 1960s, who arrived shortly after Castro's revolution, were well off and well educated. That was not the case with the next wave of Cuban immigrants. For a period of about six months in 1980, Castro lifted the government's ban on Cubans' leaving the country. Cuba's economy was still struggling at that time,

Americans of Caribbean and Central American Descent

Country of Origin	Number of People
Cuba	1,520,276
El Salvador	1,371,666
Dominican Republic	1,217,225
Jamaica	910,979
Guatemala	874,799
Haiti	762,925
Honduras	490,317
Nicaragua	295,059

Source: U.S. Bureau of the Census, 2006 estimates

and more than 125,000 Cubans left the island—the vast majority of them coming to the United States. Some left by plane but by far the largest number made the trip by boat from the Cuban port of Mariel. Cuban Americans in Florida brought boats to Mariel to pick up Cubans trying to get out. For weeks a steady stream of boats of all kinds, most of them seriously overcrowded on the return trip, went back and forth between Florida and Cuba. The event became known as the Mariel boatlift. Castro also released prisoners and mental patients at this time and put them aboard the boats as well.

For the most part, the Marielitos, as the new immigrants came to be called, were poor people leaving with little money and few possessions. Most were hard-working, honest people looking for more economic opportunity. However, the fact that a small number were released criminals led some Americans to view them all as troublemakers whom Cuba had tossed out.

Many of the Marielitos initially went to refugee camps in the United States until sponsors could help them get settled. Charities and the Cuban-American community helped many to resettle and adjust. About one in five of the Marielitos were sent to a military barracks in Arkansas while the government attempted to determine which ones might be criminals or others not allowed to stay.

Jose Salina was one of the Marielitos held in Arkansas. In a 2001 interview with the *Associated Press*, he recalled his experience: "We came here, we didn't know the language, and we didn't know what our future would be. And you had extremely violent people kept in the same place as honest people." In June 1980, such conditions led to a riot among the 21,000 Cubans being held, and the Arkansas National Guard was brought in to deal with the violence. Ultimately, some three thousand Cubans were denied admission to the United States.

Although not on anything like the scale of the Mariel boatlift, Cubans continued to try to reach Florida by boat in the late twentieth and early twenty-first centuries.

The Elian Gonzalez Custody Battle

In November 1999, a handmade boat carrying fourteen Cubans sank off the Florida coast. Only three passengers survived. One of them, Elian Gonzalez, was found tied to an inner tube and floating offshore. Elian was just five years old. His mother had drowned trying to get them both to relatives in Miami.

The fisherman who found Elian turned him over to the Coast Guard. Since Elian was picked up at sea, he should have been returned to Cuba. Instead, the boy was taken to his relatives in Florida. But there was a problem. Elian's mother had made the trip without his father's knowledge. His father was still in Cuba, and he wanted his son returned home.

Elian became the center of a bitter legal battle. His relatives in Miami argued that Elian should be granted **asylum**. They fought in court to keep the boy in Miami. But his father argued that he had a right to custody of his son and to bring him home to Cuba. In April 2000,

then–U.S. Attorney General Janet Reno ordered that Elian be returned to his father. The decision drew massive protests from the Cuban-American community in Florida. When the family refused to turn Elian over, federal agents burst into the house to take the boy away.

Elian was reunited with his father and returned to Cuba. In 2008, Elian was living in Cuba with his father, stepmother, and brothers and sisters, and he became a member of Cuba's Young Communist Union. Many people in the Cuban-American community continued to disagree with the U.S. government's decision to send him back to Cuba.

Armed federal agents find Elian Gonzalez in the Miami home of relatives.

Waves of Haitian Immigration

Haitians first began arriving in the United States in large numbers in the 1950s. Francois "Papa Doc" Duvalier (he was a medical doctor) came to power in Haiti in 1957. Duvalier was a corrupt and brutal dictator who tolerated no opposition. He ruled Haiti until his death in 1971. His private army may have killed up to 30,000 people. Thousands more decided to leave the country after he took power. Most of them were well-educated professionals, including doctors, lawyers, and teachers. Many of these people settled in such major American cities as New York, Chicago, and Boston, where they found the best job opportunities.

In 1971, Duvalier's son, Jean-Claude "Baby Doc" Duvalier, took over as ruler. Like his father, he brutally silenced anyone who opposed him. Haiti began to plunge even deeper into poverty. That brought the next big wave of Haitian immigration. This time, the people coming to the United States were poor and less educated. They didn't have the money to pay for airfare or visas. Instead, they crossed the 700 miles (1,100 kilometers) between the United States and Haiti by boat. They came to be known as boat people. In the 1970s and 1980s, perhaps as many as 80,000 undocumented immigrants from Haiti reached the United States. Many others died trying—in small boats that were old, in poor condition, and severely overcrowded. In 1981, an estimated one thousand Haitians were arriving in Florida each month. Many of the Haitian boat people settled in Miami, in a section of the city now known as Little Haiti, and in other areas in South Florida.

The flow of Haitian boat people stopped briefly in 1990. That year Jean-Bertrand Aristide was elected president. Many Haitians believed he would help the poor. But in 1991, Aristide was overthrown, and Haiti's military took over the government. Thousands of Haitians fled the country to escape the violence that followed. Some were granted refugee status by the United States. Some succeeded in landing as undocumented immigrants. Thousands were stopped by the U.S. Coast Guard, and many of these people were sent to the U.S. military base at Guantanamo Bay, Cuba. The number of boat people dropped beginning in 1994, when military rule ended and Aristide returned to power. (Haitians held at Guantanamo were returned to Haiti at that time.) In 1998, the Haitian Refugee Immigration Fairness Act made it easier for Haitians who had reached the United States to obtain U.S. government authorization to remain in the country. The early twenty-first century saw continued political unrest in Haiti—and more Haitian boat people reaching, or trying to reach, Florida.

Dominican Immigrants

The 1960s was a time of political unrest in the Dominican Republic, and this unrest made the economy worse in an already-poor country. After U.S. immigration laws changed in the 1960s, many Dominicans took advantage of the opportunity to come to the United States. What had been a very small Dominican-American community began to grow rapidly. By the 1970s, political violence had largely ended, but continuing economic problems led tens of thousands of Dominicans to immigrate. Their numbers grew to hundreds of thousands in the 1980s and 1990s. The 2000 U.S. Census counted a Dominican-American population of more than three-quarters of a million people, mostly recent immigrants; 90 percent of Dominican Americans in the year 2000 had been born in the Dominican Republic.

Most Dominican immigrants headed to New York and other nearby northeastern states. These states had few Dominican Americans before the recent wave of immigration. But they had sizable Puerto Rican populations, so the Dominican immigrants could at least find neighborhoods where there were many other Spanish speakers. Many neighborhoods have since taken on a distinctly Dominican flavor. The Washington

A small boat filled with more than 150 Haitians tries to reach the United States in the early 1990s.

35

Heights section of New York City, for example, is a hub of Dominican-American culture.

The Dominicans coming to the United States in the late twentieth century included both people with immigrant visas and undocumented immigrants seeking more economic opportunity than their native country offered.

"Wet Foot, Dry Foot"

In the first few years of the twenty-first century, the Dominican Republic's economy plunged to new lows (before economic conditions improved following the election of a new president in 2004). Many people struggled to find work and to support themselves and their families. Desperate, many decided to risk a journey by boat to try to enter the United States. A number of Dominicans headed first to Puerto Rico. Some were able to find work and stayed on the island. According to the U.S. Census Bureau, about 70,000 Dominicans were living in Puerto Rico in 2006. Most Dominican immigrants, however, continued on to the U.S. mainland.

Undocumented Dominicans trying to reach the United States by boat may pay smugglers several hundred dollars to take them onboard. They leave at night in old, rickety boats painted black or some other dark color to make them harder to spot. Often the small vessels are dangerously overcrowded. The journey can take days. "You lose your senses out there. The waves are huge," immigrant Francisco Miranda told the Associated Press in 2004. "You could pay me, and I wouldn't go again."

U.S. Coast Guard patrols try to stop undocumented immigrants from entering the United States by sea. For the most part, anyone caught at sea trying to enter the United States without a visa is shipped home. However, the U.S. government typically allows any Cuban who makes it onto dry land to stay. This is often called the "wet foot, dry foot" policy. U.S. policy is generally very different for most other undocumented immigrants, however. Haitians and Dominicans who make the same dangerous journey across the Caribbean on rafts and small boats and reach U.S. soil are usually sent home if caught by the authorities. The policy difference may stem from the continued strain in relations between the United States and Cuba and from the political influence of Florida's Cuban-American community (a large community in one of the largest U.S. states), which generally opposes the Cuban government and supports efforts by Cubans to leave the country.

Civil Wars in Central America

The 1980s brought a surge of refugees from Central America. In the late 1970s and the 1980s, El Salvador and Nicaragua were being torn apart by bloody civil wars. Many people fled in fear for their lives. Often the immigrants from these countries came to the United States seeking political asylum.

People who are under attack because of their political beliefs, religion, or ethnic background can apply for asylum, or protection. Immigrants who get political asylum are allowed to stay in the United States. During the 1980s, however, U.S. immigration policy was closely tied to cold war politics and fears of Communism.

El Salvador at this time had governments in which military leaders had a great deal of power. These governments received military and other aid from the United States to fight rebel groups, believed to be controlled by Communists, that wanted to overthrow the government and redistribute land and other wealth to the poor. Many Salvadorans sympathized with the rebels' goal of helping the poor, including a number of Roman Catholic priests. "Death squads" apparently supported by the government killed thousands of Salvadorans thought to be supporting the rebels. In 1980, the archbishop of San Salvador (El Salvador's capital city), who had criticized the government, was assassinated inside his church.

In Nicaragua, however, the situation was different. A dictator was overthrown in 1979, and a new government led by a group called the Sandinistas was set up. The United States considered this government to be Communist. In the 1980s, the United States supported rebels known as *contras* (*contra* is the Spanish word for "against") who were fighting to overthrow the Sandinistas. About 48,000 people from Nicaragua applied for political asylum from 1984 to 1990. About 25 percent of them were given asylum. The U.S. government saw them as people fleeing a Communist government. At the same time, about 45,000 people from El Salvador applied for asylum. Fewer than 3 percent of them were allowed to stay. To give them asylum would have been politically difficult. The United States

A funeral procession for six Catholic priests found murdered, apparently by government-backed assassins during El Salvador's 1980s civil war, makes its way through San Salvador.

supported the govern-ment they were fleeing. Guatemala in the late 1970s and 1980s also had military governments that fought against rebel groups believed to be controlled by Communists. Death squads in Guatemala killed thousands of people thought to be supporters of the rebels, and thousands of refugees also fled from Guatemala at this time. Many of the refugees coming to the United States were not granted asylum.

The dangers for people fleeing Central America were very real. When the U.S. government refused to let most Salvadoran (and Guatemalan) refugees stay in the country, many churches decided to help these people. Churches and other organizations across the United States formed what became known as the Sanctuary Movement. The word *sanctuary* means "shelter from harm." They gave refugees, many of whom had little money, help with finding a place

Temporary Relief

In 1998, Hurricane Mitch struck Central America. It was the deadliest hurricane to hit the region in two hundred years. The storm killed more than 11,000 people and flattened large areas of Honduras and Nicaragua. Strong winds and heavy rains washed away roads, schools, towns, homes, and crops. After the disaster, the United States relaxed its policy toward undocumented immigrants from the hardest-hit regions.

Undocumented immigrants from El Salvador, Honduras, Nicaragua, and Guatemala were given Temporary Protected Status. This allowed people to stay in the United States, even though their undocumented status was known to authorities and they would have been **deported**. Many of them no longer had homes in Central America to go back to. The U.S. government made a similar decision to temporarily stop deportations to El Salvador in 2001, after two massive earthquakes shook that country and caused severe damage.

Not everyone supported the government's decision to let known undocumented immigrants stay. Some people worried that it would encourage more undocumented immigration from Central America. Natural disasters in Central America do often bring more immigrants to the United States. People who have lost everything may decide that it is best to start a new life elsewhere.

to live, getting other necessities, and making a new life for themselves in the United States.

By doing this, the aid groups were breaking the law. In 1991, however, as a result of a lawsuit brought by organizations including American Baptist Churches USA, the government agreed to reconsider the applications for asylum of most Salvadoran and Guatemalan refugees. Then, in 1997, the Nicaraguan Adjustment and Central American Relief Act enabled Salvadoran and Guatemalan refugees to apply for the right to live permanently in the United States.

Escaping Poverty

Since the 1990s, Central American countries including El Salvador, Nicaragua, and Guatemala have had democratic governments. The newest immigrants from Central America aren't fleeing the violence of civil war. They come to the United States to escape poverty, sometimes aggravated by the devastation of natural disasters. Many of these people do not go through the process of applying for visas from the U.S. government to live and work in the United States—the application process can be complex (especially for people with very little formal education), the waits for available visas are very long, and the application fees may be beyond what many poor immigrants could afford. Instead they travel as best they can and try to enter the United States without documentation. Perhaps as many as half of all the Central American immigrants in the United States are undocumented.

The journey can take months. Immigrants hop aboard railway freight cars in the middle of the night. They wade or raft over rivers. They may pay smugglers, sometimes called **coyotes**, to help them get across the U.S. border, but the coyotes often rob the people who are paying them for safe passage. All immigrants coming overland to the United States from Central America have to pass through Mexico. Sometimes they pay smugglers to help them get into Mexico. Corrupt Mexican immigration officials may demand payment, too. People who can't pay may be beaten. Many of the immigrants who reach Mexico end up working as farm laborers in Mexican fields to make money to continue on to the United States. Mexican law is very tough on undocumented immigrants. Unlike in the United States, in Mexico they are not entitled to any

One Person's Story: Ernesto's Journey

Ernesto traveled from El Salvador through Guatemala and Mexico and entered the United States as an undocumented immigrant in the 1990s. When he arrived in Texas, he was helped by Casa Juan Diego, a nonprofit organization that assists immigrants. He told the story of his journey to the organization's newspaper:

"In El Salvador . . . employment has decreased. Because of this I became one of the thousands of Salvadorans who day by day decide to travel to the United States. [When I reached Guatemala], I shared conversations about ordinary things with other migrants who told me the places where it was best to cross, where the Immigration check points were, and thus I decided to cross to the other side of Guatemala toward Mexico. I crossed the river [into Mexico] in an inner tube. I remember that [the smugglers] said they would charge . . . ten Mexican pesos [each to help a group of us to get across]. What I didn't know was that on the other side, the same [men] would assault us with a pistol and take the little we had brought.

"We continued until we boarded [a] freight train. . . . In the early morning the train left, and with it hundreds of migrants. . . . When we came close to [the city of] Tapachula, . . . the assailants started to come out, from train car to car, assaulting the people. And if you don't give them anything, they throw you off the train.

"Upon arriving in Tonalá . . . we had to go and [beg] for food, . . . since we no longer had any money—all was robbed. After a while the shame of begging left me."

Ernesto continued traveling north through Mexico on foot and by train.

"Upon arriving in Tlaxcala, there was an immigration and army check point, and we all jumped off the train. [When another migrant jumped], he fell, [and] the wheels of the train cut his two feet. When we picked him up, he cried out, 'My feet! The train took them off!'

"[When I arrived] at a place called Huehetoca, I decided to work to put together money to continue my journey. I worked approximately six months and earned five thousand Mexican pesos. I said, with this I can make it to the [United States]. I didn't know that, upon arriving in Celaya, . . . the federal police would assault me. [T]hey found my money. And they took it from me. Then I went on without money, begging for food.

"When I arrived in San Luis Potosí to board another train that would take me to the [U.S.] border, I met other Salvadorans waiting for the train. The private police hired by the train [company] came out and asked us for money, but we didn't have any. They beat us and let us continue on our way.

"[Two days later, we] found our way to the Rio Grande. . . . We took off our clothes and crossed. In Laredo, Texas, we walked for a day until we got to where the freight train leaves. I decided to board."

Soon after, Ernesto's journey ended at a house run by Casa Juan Diego in Houston.

Some carrying water bottles, immigrants walk across the border between Mexico and Arizona.

government-provided medical care except for emergency care. Their children are not entitled to go to school. Each year, Mexico deports tens of thousands of undocumented immigrants to their home countries in Central America.

Entering the United States from Mexico is another challenge. U.S. border security has tightened a great deal in recent years. Hundreds of miles of new fencing and additional border security measures have largely cut off access to many traditional crossing points, such as those near cities in California and Texas. More undocumented immigrants are making the crossing in remote areas of the Sonoran Desert, which spans the Mexico-Arizona border. When temperatures in the desert top 125°F (52°C) in the summer months, some people literally die trying to make it across. Those who succeed may stay in Arizona, but most then spread out seeking jobs in different parts of the United States. For example, southeastern states such as Virginia, Georgia, and North Carolina have growing populations of immigrants from Central America.

A Jamaican immigrant at his clothing and music store in Miami.

CHAPTER FOUR

MAKING A NEW LIFE

Juanita Castro is the sister of former Cuban president Fidel Castro and current president Raul Castro. She fought alongside her brothers during the Cuban Revolution. However, she disagreed with her brother Fidel Castro's decision to form a Communist government. Juanita Castro left Cuba in 1964. After a brief stay in Mexico, she moved to Miami. She opened a pharmacy and became a successful businesswoman. "I have lived here longer than I have lived there," she said in a 2006 interview with *USA Today*. "I love my country, but this is my home. I belong more to this country than to my own country."

Castro's attitude is common among Cuban Americans. There are almost twice as many foreign-born as U.S.-born

Cuban Americans. Yet in surveys, most Cuban Americans identify the United States as their home country. That's unusual compared to other **Hispanic** Americans, most of whom are more likely to identify their country of origin as their homeland.

Today, many Cuban immigrants still settle in Florida, where the Cuban community is well-established. Cuban Americans provide a lot of support for new immigrants. Many see each new arrival as a small victory over the Communist government of Cuba.

The West Indian Experience

The experience of immigrants from other islands in the West Indies varies greatly, depending on who they are and where they come from. English-speaking immigrants from such former British colonies as Jamaica and the Bahamas have an advantage in that they don't have to learn a new language. However, black immigrants from former British colonies still may face racial **discrimination** when they arrive in the United States.

West Indians often form tight-knit communities and hold onto their cultural traditions. They do this, in part, to keep their heritage alive. However, it also sets them apart from the African-American community. Some immigrants see maintaining a separate identity as a way to head off some of the racism that has historically been directed toward blacks in the United States, but it sometimes also creates friction between West Indians and African Americans. Another source of friction between the two groups is that

African Americans may see the new immigrants as competition for jobs.

The Jamaican-American community includes a sizable proportion of people with high levels of education, which helps them find higher-paying jobs. According to 2006 Census Bureau estimates, more than 80 percent of Jamaican-American adults have at least a high school education, and almost one in five has a college or graduate school degree. More than 30 percent of Jamaican-American adults who are working have management or professional jobs (teacher, lawyer, or doctor, for instance). About one-quarter work in office jobs or in sales. The median family income for Jamaican Americans is more than $54,000, slightly below the figure for all U.S. families. (The median is the figure that divides a group in half—that is, half of families make more than the median, and half make less.) The Jamaican-American community also includes people who are not

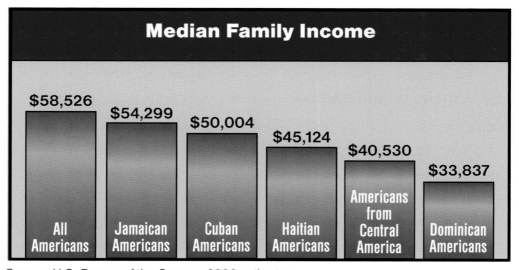

Source: U.S. Bureau of the Census, 2006 estimates

well off economically. More than 14 percent of Jamaican Americans live in poverty (as defined by the U.S. government), slightly higher than the figure of 13 percent for the total U.S. population.

Haiti is the poorest country in the Western Hemisphere. About 85 percent of Haitians cannot read or write. Many Haitian immigrants are desperate to escape the poverty (and sometimes political unrest) of their native country. However, their lack of education is an obstacle to their success once they arrive in the United States. Almost one in five Haitian Americans lives below the poverty level. Almost two in five Haitian Americans in the labor force work in service jobs (including jobs like sales clerk, waiter, or other restaurant worker), which tend to be low-paying. The median family income for Haitian Americans is more than $13,000 below the figure for all U.S. families.

Dominicans: Keeping Home Fires Burning

In general, immigrants from Caribbean countries seek to make the United States their permanent home. They are more likely to become U.S. citizens than immigrants from Central America. Dominican immigrants, however, are more likely to stay closely connected to their home country. Many say that, after making some money for themselves and their families, they plan to return to the Dominican Republic. Whether some eventually return home or not, Dominican immigrants in effect help their native country while in the United States. According to the Dominican government, immigrants send about $2 billion each year to family members back home. These payments put a significant amount of money into the struggling Dominican economy.

Long-Distance Voters

Dominican politicians often make campaign stops in Dominican neighborhoods in New York City and Miami. In 1997, the Dominican government passed a law allowing Dominican immigrants to vote abroad. Starting in 2004, in Dominican election years, Dominican immigrants have gone to polling places in, say, New York City to vote in the Dominican Republic's presidential election.

Dominican Americans send money back to relatives in their native country even though many of them are not well off by American standards. A majority of Dominican-American workers are in occupations that tend to be low-paying. Many are service workers or have jobs in manufacturing or transportation. The median family income of Dominican Americans in 2006 was under $34,000—almost $25,000 less than the figure for all U.S. families. A quarter of all Dominican Americans were living below the poverty level.

Many new immigrants live in Dominican neighborhoods. That makes settling in easier. People share the same culture and speak the same language. About half of Dominican Americans say they don't speak English very well, and more than 90 percent speak Spanish at home. That alone makes it difficult for Dominican immigrants to expand beyond their community. Yet some may not want to.

Ramona Hernandez runs the Dominican Studies Institute at the City University of New York. In 2004, she invited Dominican president-elect Leonel Fernández to speak at the institute. Fernández himself grew up in New York City. He arrived in the United States at the age of seven

Leonel Fernández, recently elected president of the Dominican Republic, is greeted by well-wishers during a 2004 visit to New York City.

and returned to the Dominican Republic after graduating from high school. He first served as president in the late 1990s and, after four years out of office, was elected president again in 2004 and 2008. "The president sees the Dominican people as one people, living in different parts of the globe," Hernandez said in an interview with the *New York Times*. Hernandez said she is one of many Dominican New Yorkers who agree with that. "I want my son, who is attending Duke University, to continue to be Dominican," she said.

Culture Clash

Many young Dominican Americans, whether they came to the United States at a young age or were born in the country, feel torn between two cultures. Their parents may want them to "be Dominican," but they may see themselves as more American. In the United States, many Americans see them as Dominicans. Yet many find that if they return to the Dominican Republic for a visit, they are viewed as Americans. All of this can add up to an identity crisis, particularly for teenagers. Some immigrant children may not feel they belong anywhere. Others decide to establish their own identity as Dominican Americans.

In the Dominican Republic, children are taught to respect their elders. Many Dominican-American teens are surprised by how much independence American children have. "I think the role of kids in society is very different," said Patricia Nuñez in an interview with the online news magazine *Worldpress.org*. Nuñez, a Dominican American, is a teacher at the Bronx High School of Science in New York City. "American kids consider themselves as vital a member of society as any adult. This is something [Dominican-American high school students] consider new and attractive."

Often, parents come to the United States first. They leave their children in the care of grandparents, who raise them with traditional Dominican values. Families may be separated for years. When the parents are finally able to bring their children to the United States, parents and children may barely recognize each other. Families can grow even more disconnected as the children adapt to life in the United States. Going to American schools, the children often learn English more quickly. And they pick up the habits and values of their fellow students. American culture, fashion, music, and dating habits are very different from more conservative Dominican traditions. Some Dominican-American parents fear they are losing control of their kids.

A teacher at a New York City school with many Dominican-American children works with a student on his English-language skills.

The Central American Experience

Immigrants from Central America come from different countries and different backgrounds. However, in the United States some Americans group them all together as Hispanics, and the immigrants may be victims of **prejudice** and discrimination. In a 2007 survey by the Inter-American Development Bank, almost four out of five of the Americans from Central America who were interviewed said they felt discrimination against Latin Americans was a growing problem. Many said they were finding it harder to get work in 2007 than in 2006. The worsening U.S. economy was probably a factor. Typically, anti-immigrant sentiments increase when the economy isn't doing well. Some people see immigrants as unfair competition for jobs. Others may believe that immigrants place too heavy a burden on social welfare programs, the health care system, and schools.

Immigrant children who don't speak English well when they first enter school often need special ELL (English-language-learner) classes, which can be an added cost for the local school system.

Almost three-quarters of Central American immigrants do not have U.S. citizenship. Many may be undocumented immigrants who are not eligible for citizenship. Non-citizens cannot vote in U.S. elections. This means that the Central American community in the United States is in a weaker position to influence public policy in ways important to the community.

Limited Opportunities

In 2006, according to U.S. Census Bureau estimates, almost half of all adult Americans of Central American origin did not have a high school diploma. More than half said they spoke English less than very well. The vast majority (91 percent) spoke Spanish at home. A lack of formal education and lack of proficiency in English limits employment opportunities. The 2007 Inter-American Development Bank survey found that almost four out of five workers were in relatively low-paying fields, working in construction or as day laborers, working as domestics (maids or child-care workers), working in the service industry at restaurants and hotels, or working in the textile industry or in agriculture.

Compared to most Americans, those of Central American origin are not economically well off. Almost one-fifth live below the poverty level. The median family income for Americans from Central America is about $40,500, or $18,000 less than the median for all U.S. families.

Cuban-American superstar Gloria Estefan at a 2008 performance.

CHAPTER FIVE

CHANGING THE AMERICAN CULTURE

People often say the United States is a melting pot. Perhaps, though, it's more like a tossed salad. Each country in Central America and the Caribbean adds a new ingredient to the mix. Sometimes those ingredients are spicy, like the hot chilies that flavor many Central American dishes. Sometimes they are sweet, like the sugar cane that grows on the Caribbean islands. Always they add something special to the culture.

Since 1988, September 15 has kicked off National Hispanic Heritage Month (which runs through October 15). September 15 is the date in 1821 when five Central American countries—Costa Rica, El Salvador, Guatemala, Honduras, and Nicaragua—declared their independence from Spain. Designated by Congress, Hispanic Heritage Month recognizes the cultures and contributions of all Hispanic Americans. Since 2006, June has been designated as Caribbean American Heritage Month, to honor the history and contributions of Caribbean Americans.

For many Americans, though, celebrating the cultures of Central America and the Caribbean is a daily event. It may take the form of enjoying foods like rice and beans, fried plantains, and spicy Jamaican patties. Or enjoying the music of Cuban-American singer Gloria Estefan. Radio stations across the United States feature Jamaican reggae and ska artists and Hispanic artists playing Latin jazz and salsa. The impact of Caribbean Americans is seen on the red carpet, when Hollywood stars parade in dazzling gowns designed by Dominican-born Oscar de la Renta.

Cuban Americans have achieved success in many areas of American life. Roberto Goizueta, who was born in Havana, headed the Coca-Cola Company, one of the largest American corporations, for almost twenty years until his death in 1997. The son of a prominent family in Cuba, Goizueta had been working for a Coca-Cola division there when he fled the island after the Cuban Revolution—with virtually no possessions except a few dollars and his first few shares of Coca-Cola stock.

Cuban-born writer Nilo Cruz won the Pulitzer Prize for Drama in 2003 for his play *Anna in the Tropics*, becoming the first Hispanic American to receive the award. The Dominican-American author Julia Alvarez spent much of her childhood in the Dominican Republic. Her novel *How the Garcia Girls Lost Their Accent* tells the story of how four sisters and their family adjust to American life after coming from the Dominican Republic to the United States.

Field of Dreams

Baseball is often called the great American pastime. But in Cuba and the Dominican Republic, people are passionate about playing ball. Many players from both countries have become stars in Major League Baseball. Cuban-born Hall of Famer Tony Perez and Dominican-born Sammy Sosa, among others, have become American baseball legends. Dominican American Alex Rodriguez, who was born in New York City but spent part of his childhood in the Dominican Republic, is one of the most outstanding hitters in Major League Baseball, though revelations in 2009 that he used banned performance-enhancing drugs earlier in his career tarnished his accomplishments. The half-brothers Orlando and Livan Hernandez both became star pitchers in the major leagues after **defecting** from

Cuban American Orlando Hernandez pitching for the New York Mets during the 2007 season.

Cuba in the 1990s. (Orlando Hernandez was briefly held in a detention center after the small boat in which he and others had left Cuba was stopped by the U.S. Coast Guard.) Many players have used their talent as their ticket to the United States. Major League Baseball teams regularly send scouts to and even run training camps located in the Dominican Republic.

Although there are a number of Cuban-American and Dominican-American baseball stars, most of the teens who pin their hopes for a future in the United States on a baseball bat wind up striking out. "When the kids are about fifteen years old, if they're strongly built, the scouts [from Major League Baseball teams] start telling them that they can be baseball players, that they can make a lot of money like Sammy Sosa. . . . So they think they can make money faster playing, doing anything except going to school," said Lala Garcia in an interview with journalist Ruben Martinez for Martinez's 2004 book *The New Americans*. At the time,

Cuban American Desi Arnaz and Lucille Ball in a 1954 episode of *I Love Lucy*.

Garcia's son Jose was living at the Los Angeles Dodgers' training camp in the Dominican Republic. The struggles of a Dominican ballplayer who comes to Iowa to play minor league baseball were the subject of the 2008 movie *Sugar*.

Hollywood Stardom

A Cuban American rose to fame in the very early days of television. Desi Arnaz, who was born in Cuba, and his wife, Lucille Ball, were stars of the hit comedy *I Love Lucy*. They also ran their own TV production studio. The show first aired in 1951. It airs in reruns to this day. On the show and in real life, Arnaz was a band leader. Cuban music was very popular at the time. People loved to dance to the rhythmic beats of salsa, meringue, mambo, and conga music. In 1997, traditional Cuban music became popular all over again with the release of the film and album *The Buena Vista Social Club*. Featuring the music of Cuban artists, the movie and album paid tribute to the Buena Vista Social Club, a private dance club and gathering place for musicians in Havana in the 1940s.

Sidney Poitier also broke new ground. Born in Miami to Bahamian parents, he was the first black actor to win an Academy Award for Best Actor, for his performance in the 1963 film *Lilies of the Field*. In 1967, he starred in the film *Guess Who's Coming to Dinner*, in which he played an African-American doctor who is engaged to a white woman. The film is about how their families react to the news that the couple plans to marry. The movie raised many issues about the obstacles an interracial couple faced

Viva America!

Actress America Ferrera puts on very large braces and a very unattractive wig for the shooting of each episode of *Ugly Betty*, a highly popular TV comedy that pokes fun at the fashion world. The show, which premiered in 2006, is based on a Colombian soap opera called *Betty la Fea* (which means "ugly Betty" in Spanish). Ferrera's parents moved to the United States from Honduras in the 1970s. America, born in 1984, is the youngest of six children, all born and raised in Los Angeles. Ferrera has also starred in two films based on Ann Brashares's popular book series *The Sisterhood of the Traveling Pants*. In 2007, Ferrera won the Emmy Award for Best Actress in a Comedy Series for her portrayal of Betty Suarez in *Ugly Betty*. Talking about the TV series in an interview with *USA Today*, Ferrera said, "What I think is successful is, it's not about stereotypes. They're not hitting piñatas every weekend. More important than having Latinos on TV is having a representation of the variations of what a Latino is."

in American society at that time.

More recently, the Honduran-born comedian Carlos Mencia has risen to stardom with humor that pokes fun at some people's **stereotypes** about Hispanic Americans. Cameron Diaz, one of the highest-paid actors in Hollywood, has a Cuban-American father. America Ferrera, the U.S.-born daughter of Honduran immigrants, makes people laugh in the title role on the TV sitcom *Ugly Betty*.

Party Time

Every March in Miami, Little Havana's Calle Ocho is the site of a

America Ferrera with her 2007 Emmy Award for her role in the TV series *Ugly Betty*.

huge street festival. The celebration of Cuban-American culture attracts up to one million people from all over. People dress in colorful costumes for a street parade; there are dance and music performances by top Latin artists. The Kiwanis Club of Little Havana started the first festival in 1978. At the time, many people viewed Cuban Americans as outsiders who stuck together and didn't interact much with non-Cubans. The festival invited everyone in Miami to come to Little Havana, learn more about Cuban-American culture, and join the fun. City residents have been partying together ever since. On March 13, 1988, a total of 119,986 people danced in a conga line down Calle Ocho, earning an entry in the book now called *Guinness World Records* for the world's longest conga line.

Political Activism and Public Office

In 2009, the U.S. Congress included six Cuban Americans, two in the Senate and four in the House of Representatives. Cuban-born lawyer Emilio Gonzalez was a foreign policy adviser to President George W. Bush and headed U.S. Citizenship and Immigration Services from 2005 to 2008.

A leading figure in the early African-American civil rights movement was W. E. B. Dubois, the U.S.-born son of a Haitian father and African-American mother. In the early twentieth century, he wrote many books about slavery and the African-American experience and spoke out for equal rights for African Americans. In 1909, he was one of the founders of the National Association for the Advancement of Colored People (NAACP), which is one of the oldest and

Colin Powell

The son of immigrants from Jamaica, Colin Powell went on to hold the highest military and foreign policy positions in the U.S. government. Powell was born in New York City in 1937, and he became an officer in the U.S. Army in 1958. He served in Vietnam twice in the 1960s, during the Vietnam War, and was injured both times. In the following years, Powell rose to the rank of general in the Army and also served in advisory positions at the Defense Department and the White House. From 1989 to 1993, he was chairman of the Joint Chiefs of Staff, the highest military position in the U.S. government. He was the first black American to hold that office. While serving as chairman, he led the U.S. military in the successful Persian Gulf War against Iraq in 1991. In 2001, President George W. Bush appointed Powell as U.S. Secretary of State. He was again the first black American to serve in that position, which he held until 2005.

still one of the leading civil rights organizations in the United States.

In 1968, Caribbean American Shirley Chisholm became the first black woman elected to Congress. Born in New York City, Chisholm was the daughter of immigrants from Barbados, and she spent part of her childhood in Barbados, living with her grandmother and going to school there. As a member of the U.S. House of Representatives for fourteen years, she was an advocate of equal rights for black Americans and for women.

Four years after her election to Congress, in 1972, Chisholm became the first black woman to run for president. "I stand before you today as a candidate for the Democratic nomination

Colin Powell speaks about national service during a 2009 public appearance.

Shirley Chisholm announces her candidacy for president in 1972.

for the presidency of the United States," she said in announcing her candidacy. "I am not the candidate of black America, although I am black and proud. I am not the candidate of the women's movement of this country, although I am a woman, and I am equally proud of that. I am not the candidate of any political bosses or special interests. I am the candidate of the people." Chisholm did not win the Democratic Party's nomination to run for president that year, and few political experts at the time expected that she would. But her pioneering candidacy could be considered an important step in a long process of opening up high political office in the United States to all Americans. By 2008, the two leading candidates for the Democratic Party's nomination to run for president were a woman, then–Senator Hillary Clinton, and an African American, then–Senator Barack Obama. And in November 2008, Obama was elected as the first African-American president of the United States.

As more immigrants from the Caribbean and Central America turn out to vote, their impact on government policies may increase. Voters here are lined up to cast their ballots in Miami in the 2008 presidential election.

CHAPTER SIX

LOOKING TO THE FUTURE

Immigrants from many countries in the Caribbean and Central America have started coming to the United States in large numbers only recently. To a large extent, the impact of these people and their descendants on American life remains to be seen. Often the newest arrivals are clustered in just a handful of major cities or other areas. They tend to have a political impact at the local level first. For example, Dominican-American children make up about 10 percent of all students in New York City public schools. Increasingly, Dominican-American parents, unhappy with the quality and services at some schools, have become active on local school boards to try to make a difference in their children's education. Similarly, Haitian Americans are starting to make their presence felt in local politics in some areas of Florida.

U.S.-Cuba Relations

The Cuban-American community is large and well established. It's a powerful presence—culturally, economically, and politically—in Florida. And government leaders in Washington, D.C., also pay close attention to its views.

As of early 2009, the U.S. government still restricted trade with Cuba, and Americans generally were not permitted to travel to Cuba. But there were some signs of change. Early 2009 legislation eased the overall trade and travel restrictions slightly, and in April 2009, the Obama administration announced that Cuban Americans could visit and send money to Cuba with virtually no limitations.

Many Cuban Americans oppose changes in U.S. policy. Others, however, would like to have closer contact with relatives on the island. Some experts believe more contact and trade could help bring about political and economic changes in Cuba.

Fidel Castro (*left*) is shown here in 2004 with his brother Raul, who later succeeded him as president of Cuba.

In 2008, Fidel Castro officially stepped down as president of Cuba (because of illness), after almost half a century in power. He was succeeded as president by his brother Raul. Some experts thought this change of government—or perhaps a later change of government to a new generation of leaders—could result in changes in Cuba's Communist system and perhaps in steps to improve relations with the United States. In that event,

At a White House ceremony in 2005, President George W. Bush signed the DR-CAFTA free trade agreement on behalf of the United States.

U.S. immigration policy toward Cubans might also change. The result could be more Cubans immigrating to the United States to join family members. On the other hand, if Cuba's economy improved, perhaps fewer Cubans would want to become immigrants and move to the United States.

Trade Agreements

Many people believe that improving the economies in poor countries in Latin America will cut down on the number of undocumented immigrants coming to the United States. In 2004, the United States and six Latin American countries completed negotiations on a new trade agreement called the Dominican Republic-Central America-United States Free Trade Agreement (DR-CAFTA). The Central American countries included are Costa Rica, El Salvador, Guatemala, Honduras, and Nicaragua. The agreement reduces or removes tariffs (taxes) on imports and exports and removes other obstacles to trade between the countries included in it. If the agreement makes it easier for companies in the Latin American countries to export products to the United States, then those companies will hire more workers. If Central American and Dominican workers have greater job opportunities—and can make decent enough wages—in their native countries, fewer people may feel the need to come to the United States.

However, the impact of DR-CAFTA, which started going into effect in 2006, may not be apparent for some time.

Immigration Reform

Immigration was a hot topic in the 2008 U.S. presidential election campaign—in particular, the large numbers of undocumented immigrants entering the United States from many places, including Central America and the Caribbean. By some estimates,

A Border Patrol truck checks some of the new fencing put up in 2008 to improve security along the U.S.-Mexico border.

as many as 12 million undocumented immigrants were living in the United States in 2008. Just about everyone agreed that U.S. immigration policy needed to be reformed. They just couldn't agree on how to do it. Many people saw still tighter border security, especially along the U.S.-Mexico border, as the best solution. Others argued that it would be impossible to completely seal U.S. borders.

Some people favored stricter enforcement of the laws that prohibit U.S. companies from hiring undocumented workers. Yet undocumented immigrants may make up a significant portion of the workforce in certain areas of the economy. They make a contribution to the American economy by their work. Some members of Congress proposed creating a temporary worker program. Such a program would give people permission to enter the United States to work for several years at a time.

Perhaps the biggest debate has been over what to do with the undocumented immigrants who are already in the United States. Some people favored increased efforts to find and deport undocumented immigrants. However, rounding up and deporting an estimated 12 million people was widely seen as virtually impossible. Also, for the U.S.-born children of undocumented immigrants, deportation poses special problems. Children born in the United States are automatically U.S. citizens. If their parents are deported, they are forced to choose between leaving their home country or living apart from their parents. To get undocumented immigrants out of a situation where they are living in hiding, some political leaders proposed giving longtime U.S. residents a path to citizenship. Other political leaders strongly opposed any such **amnesty** program, saying that it would reward people who broke the law by entering the country without authorization.

Growing Political Power

Whatever the outcomes of the ongoing immigration debate, the chances are good that Hispanic Americans (including Americans of Central American, Cuban, and Dominican origin) will help shape whatever policy develops. The Hispanic-American community is becoming increasingly politically active. In the 2008 presidential election, an estimated 10 million Hispanic Americans voted, an increase of 2.4 million over 2004. Their votes may have helped determine the election outcome in some key states. Overall, about two-thirds of Hispanic voters cast their ballots for Barack Obama. Obama, the Democratic candidate, won the state of Florida, with its large number of Cuban and other Hispanic voters. Obama also won the states of Colorado, Nevada, and New Mexico, which all have growing Hispanic populations. All four states had been won by Republican George W. Bush in 2004.

According to some estimates, by the year 2020, at least 12 percent of all Americans eligible to vote will be Hispanic. By 2040, the figure may be around 25 percent. If Hispanic Americans—and Haitian Americans, Jamaican Americans, and others—actually turn out to vote on election days, they stand to gain more control over their own future. They will also shape the future of the United States.

FACTS ABOUT AMERICANS FROM CENTRAL AMERICA

Characteristic	Americans from Central America	Percentage for Central Americans	Total U.S. Population	Percentage for U.S. Population
Total population	3,372,090		299,398,485	
Male	1,787,208	53%	146,705,258	49%
Female	1,584,882	47%	152,693,227	51%
Median age (years)	29		36	
Under 5 years old	303,488	9%	20,957,894	7%
18 years and over	2,319,265	69%	224,548,864	75%
65 years and over	121,080	4%	35,927,818	12%
Average family size	4		3	
Number of households	919,214		111,617,402	
Owner-occupied housing units	386,070	42%	74,783,659	67%
Renter-occupied housing units	533,144	58%	36,833,743	33%
People age 25 and over with high school diploma or higher	1,072,325	53%	164,729,046	84%
People age 25 and over with bachelor's degree or higher	222,558	11%	52,948,622	27%
Foreign born	2,301,544	68%	37,547,789	13%
Number of people who speak a language other than English at home (population 5 years and older)	3,068,602	91%	55,807,878	20%
Median family income	$40,530		$58,526	
Per capita income	$15,238		$25,267	
Individuals living below the poverty level	606,976	18%	38,921,803	13%

Source: U.S. Bureau of the Census, 2006 American Community Survey estimates   Note: Figures in this table do not include Belize.

FACTS ABOUT CUBAN AMERICANS

Characteristic	Cuban Americans	Percentage for Cuban Americans	Total U.S. Population	Percentage for U.S. Population
Total population	1,520,276		299,398,485	
Male	760,138	50%	146,705,258	49%
Female	760,138	50%	152,693,227	51%
Median age (years)	41		36	
Under 5 years old	91,217	6%	20,957,894	7%
18 years and over	927,368	61%	224,548,864	75%
65 years and over	288,852	19%	35,927,818	12%
Average family size	3		3	
Number of households	558,932		111,617,402	
Owner-occupied housing units	340,949	61%	74,783,659	67%
Renter-occupied housing units	217,983	39%	36,833,743	33%
People age 25 and over with high school diploma or higher	809,547	75%	164,729,046	84%
People age 25 and over with bachelor's degree or higher	280,643	26%	52,948,622	27%
Foreign born	928,817	61%	37,547,789	13%
Number of people who speak a language other than English at home (population 5 years and older)	1,200,410	84%	55,807,878	20%
Median family income	$50,004		$58,526	
Per capita income	$23,623		$25,267	
Individuals living below the poverty level	228,041	15%	38,921,803	13%

Source: U.S. Bureau of the Census, 2006 American Community Survey estimates

FACTS ABOUT DOMINICAN AMERICANS

Characteristic	Dominican Americans	Percentage for Dominican Americans	Total U.S. Population	Percentage for U.S. Population
Total population	1,217,225		299,398,485	
Male	559,924	46%	146,705,258	49%
Female	657,301	54%	152,693,227	51%
Median age (years)	30		36	
Under 5 years old	97,378	8%	20,957,894	7%
18 years and over	839,885	69%	224,548,864	75%
65 years and over	73,034	6%	35,927,818	12%
Average family size	4		3	
Number of households	363,107		111,617,402	
Owner-occupied housing units	101,670	28%	74,783,659	67%
Renter-occupied housing units	261,437	72%	36,833,743	33%
People age 25 and over with high school diploma or higher	444,044	64%	164,729,046	84%
People age 25 and over with bachelor's degree or higher	97,135	14%	52,948,622	27%
Foreign born	734,635	60%	37,547,789	13%
Number of people who speak a language other than English at home (population 5 years and older)	1,052,656	94%	55,807,878	20%
Median family income	$33,837		$58,526	
Per capita income	$13,710		$25,267	
Individuals living below the poverty level	304,306	25%	38,921,803	13%

Source: U.S. Bureau of the Census, 2006 American Community Survey estimates

GLOSSARY

abolitionist: A person opposed to slavery who works to have it ended, or abolished.

affluent: Economically well off.

amnesty: Pardoning or overlooking an action that violates the law; for example, amnesty for undocumented immigrants allows them to continue living in the United States without facing any legal penalties.

asylum: Protection granted by the government of one country to a person who has fled from extreme danger or hardship in another country.

Communist: Referring to a political and economic system (Communism) in which a powerful government owns land, factories, and other businesses and centrally plans a country's economy. People work for government-owned and government-run enterprises. The word Communist also refers to a person who is a follower of Communism.

coyotes: The informal name for smugglers who bring undocumented immigrants into the United States.

defect: To leave one's country, usually because one disapproves of that country's policies, and settle in another country.

deported: Forced to leave a country and return to one's country of origin.

dictator: A ruler who has absolute power.

discrimination: Unfair treatment of a person or group based on such characteristics as race, ethnic group, or religion.

Hispanic: A person of Latin American or Spanish descent.

immigrant: A person who travels to another country to settle there.

nationality group: People who are from, or whose parents, grand-parents, or other ancestors are from, a particular country.

prejudice: Negative judgments about a person or a group based on such things as race, religion, ethnic group, or economic status.

quota: Maximum number or amount; immigration quotas refer to fixed maximum numbers of people who are permitted to enter a country each year.

refugee: Someone who seeks or takes shelter in a foreign country, especially to avoid war, political persecution, or religious persecution in his or her native country.

stereotypes: Commonly held, often negative, ideas about the characteristics of an entire group of people. Stereotypes do not take into consideration the individual differences among people belonging to any group.

Summit of the Americas: One of a series of meetings between the United States, Canada, and Latin American countries to promote cooperation and development in the Western Hemisphere.

undocumented immigrants: Immigrants who enter and remain in the United States without obtaining the permission and paperwork required by U.S. law.

visa: A document that indicates a person has permission to enter the United States and to remain either permanently or for a certain period of time.

TO FIND OUT MORE

Further Reading

Anderson, Dale. *Cuban Americans*. Milwaukee, WI: World Almanac Library, 2007.

Foley, Erin, and Rafiz Hapipi. *El Salvador*. New York: Marshall Cavendish Benchmark, 2006.

Foley, Erin, and Leslie Jermyn. *Dominican Republic*. New York: Marshall Cavendish Benchmark, 2006.

Senker, Cath. *The Debate About Immigration*. New York: Rosen Publishing, 2008.

Sheehan, Sean, and Leslie Jermyn. *Cuba*. New York: Marshall Cavendish Benchmark, 2006.

Websites

http://www.caribbeanamericanmonth.org
The official website for Caribbean American Heritage Month includes information on Caribbean-American culture and heritage.

http://www.cjd.org/stories/stories.html
This website for Casa Juan Diego, an organization that helps immigrants, including undocumented immigrants, offers stories of individuals who emigrated from Central America to the United States.

http://www.factmonster.com/spot/hhm1.html
The Fact Monster website has information about Hispanic heritage, language, and culture, as well as links to reports from the U.S. Census Bureau.

http://lcweb2.loc.gov/frd/cs/cshome.html
The Library of Congress Country Studies website offers information about the countries in Central America and the Caribbean.

http://www.npr.org/news/specials/polls/2004/immigration
This National Public Radio report on Immigration in America includes interviews with immigrants.

BIBLIOGRAPHY

The author found these sources especially helpful when researching this volume:

Barbassa, Juliana. "Kids of Illegal Immigrants Forced to Choose When Parents Deported." *Associated Press*, April 3, 2007.

Holmes, Steven A. "Damage in Central America Stirs Debate on Immigrants." *New York Times*, November 25, 1998.

Illegal Immigration: Border Crossing Deaths Have Doubled Since 1995; Border Patrol's Efforts to Prevent Deaths Have Not Been Fully Evaluated. Government Accountability Office, August 2006. http://www.gao.gov/new.items/d06770.pdf.

Martinez, Ruben, and Joseph Rodriguez. *The New Americans*. New York: The New Press, 2004.

Ostine, Regine. *Caribbean Immigrants and the Sociology of Race and Ethnicity: Limits of the Assimilation Perspective*. University of Michigan, Spring 1998. http://www.rcgd.isr.umich.edu/prba/perspectives/spring1998/rostine.pdf.

Ramos, Jorge. *The Latino Wave: How Hispanics Will Elect the Next American President*. New York: HarperCollins, 2004.

Rubio-Goldsmith, Raquel, et al. *A Humanitarian Crisis at the Border: New Estimates of Deaths Among Unauthorized Immigrants*. Immigration Policy Center, February 2007. http://www.immigrationpolicy.org/index.php?content = B070201.

Special Source Issue: Central America. Migration Information Source, April 2006. http://www.migrationinformation.org/issue_apr06.cfm.

Survey of Mexican and Central American Immigrants in the United States. Multilateral Investment Fund, Inter-American Development Bank, August 8, 2007. http://www.iadb.org/news/docs/remitmex.pdf.

Notes:

Chapter 3:

Page 42: "In El Salvador . . . employment has decreased. . . ." *Houston Catholic Worker*, Vol. XV, No. 8, December 1995. http://www.cjd.org/stories/elsalv.html. Reprinted with permission.

All websites were accessible as of April 7, 2009.

INDEX

Page numbers in **boldface** are illustrations, tables, and charts.

About the Series Consultant

Judith Ann Warner is a Professor of Sociology and Criminal Justice at Texas A&M International University (TAMIU), located in Laredo, Texas, near the U.S.-Mexico border. She has specialized in the study of race and ethnic relations, focusing on new immigrants to the United States and their social incorporation into American society. Professor Warner is the editor of and contributed a number of essays to *Battleground Immigration* (2009), a collection of essays on immigration and related national security issues. Recognition of her work includes the 2007 Distance Educator of the Year Award and the 1991 Scholar of the Year Award at TAMIU.

About the Author

Jayne Keedle was born in England. She spent two years in Mexico City before immigrating to the United States at age sixteen. After graduating from the University of Connecticut with a degree in Latin American Studies, she worked as a newspaper journalist and then as an editor for *Weekly Reader* classroom magazines. She lives in Connecticut with husband, Jim, and stepdaughter, Alma. As a freelance writer and editor, she has written a number of books for young adults. Her books in the New Americans series are her first for Marshall Cavendish Benchmark.